THE METHOD INVESTOR

A Direct, No-Nonsense Approach to Personal Finance

JASON KEITH

First edition April 2021

Book cover design by: ebooklaunch

ISBN 978-1-7370287-0-3

www.themethodinvestor.com

For my mother who deserves all the credit but never asked for any and my father who gave me the only creative DNA I have in my body.

And for those who have been on the wrong side of capitalism, time to jump the fence.

Table of Contents

Introduction

———— ❦ ————

"That is only for rich people, not people like us."

I was around thirteen years old when I heard that phrase from my mother. Growing up in Southern California, my life was uncomplicated and fun. Surfing in the morning and skiing in the afternoon. Paradise for a young kid.

I worried our little three-bedroom apartment might collapse in an earthquake, but it was only two miles to the beach. Perhaps a decent trade-off.

I never thought much about money.

However, the older I got, the more I noticed that money was everywhere. It became particularly noticeable during high school. It was not uncommon for classmates to get a brand-new Volkswagen Scirocco or a fixed-up Karmann Ghia for their sixteenth birthday. Nor was it uncommon for classmates to have a boat docked in the backyard of their Huntington Harbor home.

My sister and I were thrilled to have our cool $1,500 Volkswagen Bugs, but I kept wondering where all this money came from.

I was interested in what a stock was.

I had found a small book on our bookshelf about securities, and I had not known what that was. I read through it without understanding anything, but it certainly piqued my interest. I thought it was just a way to make free money.

It sounded cool to "own stocks" and use terms like "Wall Street" and "portfolio."

These were the times before the Internet existed. The only way to learn anything was to visit the library. Of course, finance books were very confusing. They were technical and way over my head. I could not use Google or YouTube to look up "stock basics."

I thought the school classroom would be the place. Everyone needs to know how to get free money, I thought. Certainly, one of my teachers would have this as part of their curriculum. As I got to middle school and on to high school, I kept waiting. My investing class never happened. I barely learned what a savings account was.

Money is at the root of many things: divorces, access to quality healthcare, affluent or poor neighborhoods, good schools or bad schools, and so on.

Fair or not, it just is. Money has a major effect on the quality of our lives. Of all the things we should have been taught, investing should have been near the top of the list. Simply put, without this knowledge and the ability to execute that knowledge, one will get left behind.

The burden of securing a financial future continues to shift toward the individual. As this happens, the middle class continues to erode. What created a comfortable life before is no longer guaranteed by working full time. The key to a secure financial life is not in the amount of money you make; it is in the amount of assets that you acquire.

You need to consistently purchase things that put money in your pocket, not take it out. In other words, you need to own things that other people are paying for. For most people, investing is the most straightforward option.

The good news: there is nothing difficult about investing. Technology has made investing incredibly simple. The education curve is much smaller than it was for me back in school. What it takes now is a simple plan to follow and action.

Envision a lengthy road trip.

Think of a destination and then a plan to get there. We need to buy gas, or it is going to be a short trip. We must think about contingencies if things do not go as planned.

We also hope to enjoy the journey.

Financially, you are on this trip in your life right now, in one way or another. Unfortunately, some never start the trip. Others take shortcuts and eventually get lost or just turn around and go home. Some make it all the way to the destination as planned. They sit on the porch and reminisce about how great their trip was. They officially made it.

You can take the trip that leads to financial freedom. You just need a simple pattern to follow that leads to the desired destination.

That is what this book is about.

The Method is an investment strategy that is designed to help people achieve financial freedom. The fundamentals are based on purchasing income-producing securities without taking on excessive risk and fees.

Let us get this important part out into the open.

I am not a financial advisor and do not advertise myself as such. I am simply a self-taught investor who has had success with a particular style of investing and thinks it would benefit others. The views and opinions in this book are educational in nature. How you use any of this information is entirely up to you.

The Method Investor is divided into two parts.

The first part contains principles related to building wealth.

The second part contains the specific, step-by-step method for designing your investing portfolio.

Section I

Principles

Storm Clouds

A Major Storm Is Brewing

You are going to need to find shelter.

When it comes to building wealth for our future years, the situation is getting a little dire. Consider the current challenges in America today with retirement planning:

Social Security is projected to run out of money by 2034. In fact, benefit statements now include the following disclaimer:

Your estimated benefits are based on current law. Congress changed the law in the past and can do so at any time. The law governing benefit amounts may change because, by 2035, the payroll taxes collected will be enough to pay only about 80 percent of scheduled benefits.

Pension plans are not doing much better. According to The Pew Charitable Trusts, a nonprofit civil watch group, public sector pensions face a trillion-dollar shortfall.

The Central States Pension Fund is a stunning example

of how challenging things have gotten. Here is the reality of the situation taken from a recent CNBC op-ed:

The Central States Pension Fund, one of the largest multi-employer pension plans, is expected to go insolvent in just five years. Not only would this directly harm hundreds of thousands of workers and retirees, with compounding effects on the children, spouses, and parents they support, but it would also result in a crippling domino effect on the US economy.

Corporate pensions are even worse if that is possible. They check in at two trillion dollars short.

In the past, we did not have to worry as much about retirement.

The shelter was built for you, typically, by Social Security or by a defined benefit plan either in the public sector or corporate pensions. The government or the company (or union) you worked for handled your retirement security. You put in your time, money came out of your paycheck, and promises were made—promises once kept.

Promises are not being kept anymore. There are many reasons why—two of the biggest are mismanagement and looting.

A simple analogy will help explain how this works.

Mr. Smith is an investment advisor for XYZ's public

pension plan. His job is to invest the pension funds (your money) in a way that produces the highest return without adding excessive risk. He is paid very well to do this, along with a team of about ten who assist him. Guaranteed high salary, often regardless of performance.

One year, Mr. Smith makes 6.8% yearly return in the market, and the average balanced fund of stocks and bonds makes 9.5%. Mr. Smith has lost a lot of money this year. Meanwhile, the pension plan needs to cover the "losses." This equals more talk about cuts. Cuts for you and me. Mr. Smith has some difficult discussions with the Board of Directors regarding his returns. In order to keep his high-paying job, he decides he needs to take more risks. More risk means the *potential* for higher returns.

He calls his good friend, Ms. Jones. Ms. Jones owns a hedge fund. Basically, a hedge fund is an investment firm that can play outside of the normal rules and hold riskier investments. Ms. Jones is brilliant and can nearly promise a 14% return. Her management fees, however, are very high compared to standard mutual funds. It's expensive to do what she does but worth it to Mr. Smith if it all works out. He will be the shining star in the end if he can produce higher returns for the pension fund.

Unfortunately, life happens.

The stock market falls due to lots of bad news in the world. Ms. Jones' hedge fund sinks like a rock. Because she borrowed lots of money to inflate her investments, the losses are staggering. Through all the chaos, two people got paid—the investment manager and the hedge fund manager. They kept moving the shells around the investments and "looted" lots of money.

It's amazing how many people and companies get paid millions of your dollars by playing this game.

Here's a recent quote from *Market Watch*:

Why do they keep doing it? Why do pension fund trustees keep doing this and falling for one of the oldest games in the business? The $4.8 billion pension fund of New York's Metropolitan Transportation Authority just became the latest to sue a hedge-fund manager after losing hundreds of millions of dollars in complicated financial vehicles that maybe nobody could understand. The MTA joins a list of woebegone pensions suing German financial giant Allianz over its "Structured Alpha" funds, which collapsed in the market turmoil earlier this year, wiping out 97% (yes, really) of investors' capital. The MTA says it had $330 million invested in the fund.

Get ready. Here comes the letter in the mail that says, "Due to unforeseen movement in the market, we are forced to decrease your monthly pension payment by 15%."

Such garbage.

Mismanagement and looting. It happens every day in the

pension world. Meanwhile, hardworking Americans pick up the pieces. That leaves you and me to fend for ourselves. We need to build our own shelter. The questions are, how do we build that shelter, and what should it look like?

Typically, you cannot control an incoming storm, but in this case, you can. It is not difficult to dissipate the storm before it has a chance to hit your retirement years. You just need to have the right investment plan in place and be consistent in building it.

While reality stares us in the face, we need to be careful of fear. Fear is a major driver of our decision-making. We fear that we've started preparing too late; we fear that we will lose money if we invest in stocks; we fear learning about investing; we fear that we will not have enough.

Let me offer this: set the fear aside. There is nothing complicated about investing. It is possible to have adequate income in retirement. We just need to supplement the income we are planning on. And let me offer some further encouragement: recent studies have shown the situation might not be as bad as it seems.

Nearly eight in ten retirees tell Gallup they have enough money to live comfortably. Eighty-one percent of recently polled retirees described their retirement as either good or better than their pre-retirement years.

It is fair to state that Americans are not saving enough. However, we need to keep one thing in perspective.

Retirement planning might be a lot like building your dream home. Everyone's idea of that is a little different.

Some people dream of a warm climate, a big home, and lots of grandchildren. Others are taking advantage of the new FIRE movement: retiring early and living on minimal income in a tiny home. One outcome is not better than the other, but this difference is something that you need to think about. You need to have a general idea of what your retirement will look like.

Suze Orman says I need five million to retire. A recent Dave Ramsey blog says one million is a "good start." My opinion is different than that of many others in this industry. You do not need a million dollars to retire, but you do need a plan.

That plan should be built around a simple investment strategy that focuses on cash flow to supplement your other retirement income. Stick to the plan and execute it to the best of *your ability*.

Money grows money. The more you invest, the more you make. That is the simple way to build wealth. Focus on that investing concept, and regardless of your income, status, and circumstances, you will have a life of freedom.

"Money grows money" is such an important statement; I will repeat it throughout this book.

The Dramatic Shift To The Individual

Life has changed dramatically in terms of preparing for a financial future.

There has been a dramatic shift to individual responsibility in building a retirement nest egg. This is and will continue to be a major challenge. Unfortunately, the days of the government and your employer providing your retirement income are fading quickly.

When things get tough, one of the first things employers do is eliminate matching contributions to employees' retirement funds—and that is assuming your employer even provides matching anymore. Lots of people today work in the "gig economy," and 401(k)s are simply not an option— let alone a company giving you free money.

Unfortunately, saving money for our future life is not really in the American DNA, at least not for most people, because there is nothing immediately tangible in doing so. Furthermore, advertising and consumerism naturally make saving, itself, a challenge. Americans are constantly bombarded with messages to spend instead of save. It is also difficult for many people to invest for their future. If saving is not done automatically, bills and life will get in the way. There will always be something to buy or pay for.

Due to many factors, the middle class is evaporating, and most families fit there. The US has always been a nation of haves and have nots, but these statuses seem evermore outside of an individual's control.

Job security is nonexistent for most. Approximately 74% of employees are considered "at will," meaning they can be fired without cause at any time.

Out-of-pocket healthcare costs are cutting big holes in family budgets. Premiums for family health insurance coverage increased by approximately 54% between 2009 and 2019. Employer costs increased by 48%, while employees contributed 71% more toward the cost of their healthcare premiums than in 2009.

There is also a massive shift in the workplace. Traditional full-time work is being replaced by independent freelancing income from multiple sources. Retirement accounts are rarely part of that structure.

The odds seem stacked. But you cannot get wealthy by dreaming. It takes action. Someone must break the chain and do things differently. That someone is you. Here is an interesting observation. If you look up what people desire most out of life, three things seem to be at the forefront:

Happiness

Money

Freedom

Yet, the actions we take in our daily lives do not often match these desires.

First, happiness is nearly impossible to define.

Most of us never get there because we do not know what the hell it is. And if we are lucky enough to know what it is, it changes in a heartbeat. Happiness is pretty elusive.

Joy is a much better destination. It is different than happiness because it contains the following definition: the emotion evoked by the prospect of possessing what one desires. Translation: you do not have to have everything right now; you just need to be working toward it. As your prospects grow, so does your joy.

Second, money is 100% controllable. It is all based on decision-making. If you say, "No, it is not because I do not make enough," you must get past that. Figure it out.

Freedom is commonly attached to money, and for good reason. In our society, money creates freedom because it allows you to make choices. Joy, money, and freedom—you can create joy, and you can create money. Together, those create freedom. It's a great road map.

You also must find a balance between living life and financing your future. Like most things in life, the sweet spot is somewhere in the middle. Efforts must be made on both ends, but the activity of creating wealth should outweigh the rest of your actions.

Another way to think about this comes from one of my favorite quotes:

"Never give up what you want most for what you want today." — *Neal Maxwell*

Life is a game.

Your financial life is a major part of that game, and lots of factors block your pawn from moving forward. Because individuals now bear the responsibility for their futures, it is critical to play and continue playing the game.

Stop heading toward financial jail. Every opportunity you get, make a payment to your future.

Critical Investment Lessons
Cash Flow First

·————— ❧ —————·

Cash flow is often associated with a business. It is the inflow and outflow of money.

Cash is a requirement for paying employees, purchasing inventory, growing the business, and paying taxes. Successful companies focus on generating cash because their future and that of their employees depend on it. As you can probably relate, not every day in the business world is going to be sunny. Cash is what gets businesses through difficult hurdles.

If you think this sounds a lot like life, you would be correct. Your life is very similar to a business when it comes to cash flow. You have "employees." Perhaps they are your children or others you care for—certainly yourself. You purchase inventory daily to live. Taxes: self-explanatory. And having additional income to invest in "growing the business"—absolutely.

Your financial future is your business.

When it comes to investing, I preach cash flow first and capital appreciation in the background. There are several reasons for this. Let me start with the first one. Cash is king. It always has been and always will be. Think of it this way: the paycheck that you receive for working is essentially cash. It allows you to buy life's necessities. If you received shares of stock every two weeks, it would be valuable, but not practical for everyday living.

There are other great examples of this. When you lose a job or get laid off, unemployment is your lifeline. Perhaps you become disabled and have insurance to cover that. It's the same concept.

Retirement is just like this too.

Expenses may be lower, but they do not stop. Imagine an extra three hundred, five hundred, or a thousand dollars that come as a monthly check and can supplement existing income such as Social Security. It is the difference between living comfortably or simply spending your nest egg and hoping it does not run out.

Most people invest with the goal of achieving a certain net worth, while some figure out what just sounds familiar. One million comes to mind because that always seems to be "the number." It may be more or less.

Typically, this figure is just an arbitrary one—something that you read in an article or have seen on television. It is important, however, to understand that achieving a net worth does not necessarily mean that it will last or that you will be able to enjoy the lifestyle you want. Your financial plan needs to provide for ongoing income; at the end of the day, what matters is how much you must spend every month.

Another important discussion around your net worth in retirement involves understanding what exactly goes into that equation. Financial advisors often factor other important assets into net worth, the largest of which might be your house.

Here is the problem.

Your primary household is an illiquid asset. It is certainly valuable but does not provide cash flow for you to live on (excluding reverse mortgages). If your goal is to retire with half a million dollars, but your house that you plan on staying in is three hundred thousand of that, then you are going to have a problem.

It is a popular idea, but I am not a big believer in paying your house off in lieu of other investments.

Paying off a mortgage prior to retirement is a huge benefit, but not if it is at the expense of compound interest in your portfolio. If you do pay it off, it is still an illiquid asset. You live in it. It does not pay for your medications or cable bill in retirement.

How should you build cash flow for retirement?

There are plenty of options but not all are good. As with any investment, there is an important balance between getting a return on your investment and risk. The edges are not a great place to be. Bank CDs, savings, and money market accounts let you sleep at night, but they also let you starve in retirement. At the opposite end, day trading and "hot tips" are worse. You will not sleep at night. You will probably starve and be tired—not a great combination.

A measured approach is what you are looking for. Your approach should involve investment in strong companies that tend to dominate their market, enough diversification to be protected, and low volatility. Most importantly, these companies should pay you directly for owning a piece. This type of investment portfolio will generate cash every month that can be reinvested during your working years and will be available to you during retirement.

Keep People Out Of Your Pocket

Be religious about this.

Other than consistently investing in your portfolio, this is a close second for achieving financial freedom.

Some things rob your potential to create wealth. Of course, we must spend money on things, and there are many things that provide value to us. Figuring out what provides value is a big decision. That determination is one of the keys to building wealth. We must know what to spend on.

I realize that most of the businesses I interact with have one goal, and that is to separate my earned income into their earned income. It is capitalism. It is a great thing if I am on the correct side of the capitalism game.

In order to build wealth, I must share in the financial benefits that these companies create.

What about spending?

Sure, find ways to reduce it, but it is important not to take this to an extreme. I do not advocate living in a shack with beans and rice for dinner every night. In fact, I am not a huge fan of budgeting because of the stress that comes with it. For most people, it is nearly impossible to follow. I'm also not suggesting that people become cheapskates. Stiffing your server, bartender, or hairdresser is not the way to build wealth.

It is equally important, however, not to be naive, especially in the financial and consumer world. People get robbed every day by sales techniques. It is just reality. Salespeople are not all bad, but think of why they are hired by their company. It's not necessarily for your benefit.

You do not need people telling you how great something is for you. How can someone who just met you on the car lot possibly know what is great for you? They do not even know your name. People who build wealth figure that out on their own.

The importance of learning about and handling your own money cannot be overstated. It is the difference between building wealth or simply handing a big portion of your future income to someone else. A significant part of building wealth is keeping people out of your pocket.

It Is Not Luck, It Is Execution

There is nothing particularly difficult about building wealth.

It is not a function of luck or the amount of money people make. It is 100% execution and commitment. You must give up on the dream of winning the lottery and have a plan that will get you to the destination.

Do you want to be wealthy? Think water.

When you start investing, it is like a dripping faucet. Perhaps you begin buying shares in your 401(k) or in an IRA account. And then nothing terribly exciting happens. The amount in your account is small, and any type of return, even if it is big, is not visible.

Twenty percent, which is a great return, might be worth about fifty or a hundred dollars in a small account. People see that and get discouraged. It is understandable. Instant gratification kicks in, and it is a tough pill to swallow. You expect big things to happen. Because you made an effort to invest money, you begin to think that it really does not work.

Buying the new Land Rover offers a lot more satisfaction because it is immediate. Here is where some people quit. Things just do not happen fast enough.

It's a huge mistake.

If you continue to add to your account on a consistent basis, your account will eventually become a small creek. The money you make through investment growth and dividends will increase. You will be able to see the "flow."

Eventually, your creek becomes a river of money. There will be lots of volume. Investment returns are worth much more and continue to compound over and over. At this stage, you are actively building wealth. You have simply invested money on a regular basis and allowed time to help. This is all very doable, especially for the reward it brings.

Ultimately, the flow becomes so great that it will overflow the riverbanks. Once here, you have reached the financial pinnacle.

Why?

Because you now have choices that equal financial freedom. You can continue to add to your account and let it continue to overflow. Or you can create the dam at this point, save your principal amount, and live on the money that it creates. Either way, once you arrive at this point, you have made it.

However, we all must determine the stage at which the river overflows. It is a personal decision based on many factors, but it is still a decision you must think about.

Remember the most valuable law when it comes to investing. **Money makes money. More money makes more money.**

It is simply the concept of compound interest. No wonder Albert Einstein called it the most powerful force in the universe. Put this statement on your refrigerator. It will make you rich.

Once you start with a dripping faucet, you are on the path to financial freedom—if you stick to it consistently.

A Secret Addiction

You need an addiction.

Choose an addiction to investing.

My life truly changed from a financial perspective when I got addicted to investing. It is more powerful than the feeling of consumerism. Trust me. Nothing is more impactful for your mental state (financially) than watching your nest egg grow. Your life changes.

Labor = money. Money = investing. Investing = wealth. Wealth = freedom. The road is straightforward.

It is unbelievably sad to think of someone laboring for forty to fifty years and having very little financially to show for it. It is a tragedy of epic proportions, but it is incredibly common.

Your labor must stand for something.

For a lot of people, it is dinner at Benihana on a Friday night. I love Benihana too, but that is not it. You must pay yourself first. Always. And you need to be addicted to it. In fact, you have really made it when you invest so often and regularly that it is practically an automatic response. You get extra dollars in your bank account, and investing is the first thing you think about.

Addiction is an interesting word to use when it comes to investing money and building wealth. Many professionals would say that an addiction can only be negative.

The first definition of addiction, according to Merriam-Webster, is the following:

A *compulsive, chronic, physiological or psychological need for a habit-forming substance, behavior, or activity having harmful physical, psychological, or social effects and typically causing well-defined symptoms (such as anxiety, irritability, tremors, or nausea) upon withdrawal or abstinence: the state of being addicted.*

Sounds very negative and familiar. But look at the second definition:

A strong inclination to do, use, or indulge in something repeatedly.

This is the definition I am referring to. Those who get addicted to building wealth will build it.

Low Beta = Moat. Why It Matters

The goal of this book is to be as nontechnical as possible, but what I will describe next is an important piece of investing.

One of the primary things I am interested in when looking at a stock is its beta value. Beta is a fancy word that simply refers to the volatility of a stock. When the market moves up and down, stocks move with it, but at different rates (depending on the stock).

Stocks with higher volatility are very exciting. They have great potential at appreciation. Stories are full of people who purchased the newest tech start-up and struck it rich.

Think new companies, biotech stocks, Silicon Valley.

No thanks. Most investors cannot stomach the ups and downs. Add me to that list. The risk to me is not worth the potential reward. Your goal should be building retirement income, which is a process. If you take the right steps, it is a lot more automatic than gambling.

Also, remember: the fear of loss is much greater than

the excitement of a gain. Human nature nearly guarantees you will sell at the wrong time. You'll experience the first major dip and sell out. You'll have bought high and sold low.

Warren Buffett would kick you out of his club.

Stocks that have a lower beta value are not as exciting, and that is a good thing.

Union Pacific Railroad is probably not going to take over the world with the newest way to transport chemicals by drones, but they are excellent at what they do. They also make lots of money, which is good if you own the stock. Their beta value hovers around 1.0. That means there are not a lot of ups and downs—just growth over time and cash to shareholders.

I prefer my portfolio to have stocks with beta values between 0 and 1.0. The biggest reason is not just lower volatility, but it tells me they have a monopoly around their business model. Or to put it another way: they have a moat around the castle.

If the drawbridge does not come down by mistake (bad management), competitors stand little chance of breaching the stone castle of cash flow.

Low volatility is what I would call "good sleeping weather" in terms of watching your stock picks. Less anxiety equals buy and hold and no emotional mistakes.

Financial Advising (Or Lack Thereof)

Is Your Advisor Really Advising You?

Hopefully, the answer is yes, but it is not always the case. Unfortunately, the horror stories are many.

Financial advisors may have your best interest at heart, but at the end of the day, their goal is to get your money into their possession. Anyone telling you differently is not being truthful.

It is estimated that financial service companies spend approximately forty billion dollars a year worldwide on advertising.

You read that correctly—forty billion dollars to get your money under their management. For financial advisors, marketing is everything in achieving their goal. Often, that marketing is geared toward showing the consumer the best possible return data. In other words, they'll display shiny objects that attract attention. It is not always reality.

Of course, financial advisors cannot promise great returns. It has been said many times, but it bears repeating: "Past performance is no guarantee of future results."

People are creatures of habit. Change is difficult, and advisors bank on this. Once your finances are in someone's hands, they tend to remain in that spot. You will probably get lots of "good news" from your advisors, even when the market is down. The fees that you pay are often hidden from view. That is purposeful. Most advisors will charge you a percentage of your portfolio and perhaps additional brokerage/management fees—guaranteed.

Imagine how exciting it is to wake up at the end of the year and open your statement, only to find that you have lost ten percent for the year, just like everyone else. But you still paid your advisor fees regardless of performance.

You lose money, and you pay anyway.

It is kind of like going to a restaurant, never getting your meal, and being asked to leave a tip.

Stocks and bonds will go up and down the same regardless of who placed the transaction. It just costs you more money if someone does that for you and continually charges you to keep it.

Building wealth is dependent upon understanding this statement.

How about honesty in the industry? Keeping financial advisors and stockbrokers honest continues to be a challenge.

Federal regulators decided to do something about it. Regulation Best Interest (also known as Reg BI) was passed in June 2019. It established a "best interest" standard of conduct for broker-dealers and associated persons when they make a recommendation to a retail customer of any securities transaction or investment strategy involving securities, including recommendations of types of accounts.

It's a nice effort, but it has very few teeth.

Financial companies who stand to lose money by Reg BI want nothing to do with it other than fight it tooth and nail. They are lining up at every courthouse in the nation to defeat it.

Let us back up a little just to emphasize how difficult it has been to change this industry. Prior to Reg BI, there was another effort to hold all financial professionals responsible.

The Department of Labor attempted to establish what was known as the fiduciary rule, which would have prevented professionals giving retirement advice from concealing any potential conflicts of interest and ensured they disclose all fees and commissions in simple dollar terms to their clients.

It meant full transparency. As soon as those who spend

the forty billion in marketing showed up, it was dead on arrival.

In March 2018, The Fifth Circuit Court of Appeals, based in New Orleans, vacated the fiduciary rule in a 2-to-1 decision, saying it constituted "unreasonableness," and that the Department of Labor's implementation of the rule constitutes "an arbitrary and capricious exercise of administrative power."

Really?

Here is how a Wall Street professional sums it up:

"Wall Street has deep pockets in place to protect their interests, unfortunately not so for the consumer. The large financial institutions that do not have a fiduciary standard would stand to lose a large chunk of their business if the fiduciary rule were in place."

In simple English, it is legal for financial professionals to take advantage of you. Unfortunately, it will continue.

According to the Department of Labor, conflicts of interest in retirement advice cost American families an estimated seventeen billion dollars a year. Again, is your advisor really advising you or selling you a relationship that may not have your best interest at heart?

Enough doom and gloom.

When it comes to financial advisors, I think the name

says it all. They should be doing just that—advising you. They set up the direction, i.e., the plan if you will. And when it comes to that process, many of them can be worth everything their credentials advertise. Financial decisions are not always simple. There are times when you will want the advice of a professional.

If you are in the market for a financial advisor, all is not lost. Many financial professionals are in strong agreement that they must put their client's interests first.

You are looking for a key word: fiduciary.

Be certain that your advisor has the designation of a fiduciary advisor. If you are not sure, just ask. They should be happy to show you their required SEC Form ADV Part 2.

My position on this is straightforward when it comes to building wealth. Financial advisors want your money. Sometimes you need their advice. Paying for that advice is worth gold. Executing that advice on your own is worth lots more gold. They advise, you execute. Keep your money in your pocket.

Monkeys, Darts and Stocks

Sometimes I feel dumb.

If only I bought stock in Apple, Tesla, and Amazon years ago.

Everyone seems to be great at picking stocks. I hear it every day on the radio. I see it on bookshelves at Barnes & Noble. Jim Cramer's stocks always have a "Boo-Yah" attached to them. Can all these people be that great at picking investments? The answer appears to be no.

Enter monkeys.

Come to find out, monkeys are a lot better at building wealth—at least in principle. Multiple studies have been done to determine if random selections of stocks can beat the professionals. The answer is a resounding yes.

I assume it was a little difficult for monkeys to explain how undervalued Walmart stock was or the level of debt on the latest Apple balance sheet. Researchers used darts instead of actual monkeys. The hypothesis was simple. Randomly picked stocks would outperform the best investment professionals. Tape a list of stocks listed in the NYSE to the wall. Throw twenty darts. Track the companies that you "hit" and compare them to the top portfolio managers' picks.

In study after study, the results were not even close.

The stocks chosen by throwing darts outperformed the professionals by 15-20%—some studies even showed the result as closer to 30%.

Amazing. What does this mean for you and me? Should we just throw darts? Can we pick random stocks and be successful?

Not exactly. The problem with throwing darts is that it does not consider risk and dividends (cash). I like darts that purposely land on strong companies with stable and increasing dividend history. I do not have to worry about zigzagging along the road to my destination.

Think of it this way.

I have no idea if Coca-Cola stock is going to go up or down in the short term. Nobody does. But I do know that they are going to pay me cash every three months, regardless. Over time, the chance of the stock growing is historically very high. We must consider cash flow first (reinvested), with capital appreciation in the background.

As monkeys show us, picking the "perfect stocks" is not what you should be concerned about. That should at least calm your mind a little. You do not need to be perfect, nor feel like you have missed out. You do need strong companies that dominate their market and pay you cash.

What about the portfolio managers with whom we entrust our financial future?

Professionals have a difficult time picking winning stocks. They tend to overestimate their abilities. If we all understood the stock market and its direction, we would not have to worry about winning the Powerball. Professionals struggle to beat the random throwing of darts but will convince you through their marketing skills that they can. And guess what? Many are well-off primarily because of the fees they charge, not because they have figured out the market.

It is very difficult to build wealth if we constantly think we have some special investing knowledge that no one else has. It is also difficult to build wealth if we are paying someone else to do the same.

Think about it. Do not confuse luck for strategy. Luck will run out eventually, with expensive results. We must follow a pattern that has a specific goal in mind, hold it, and add money to it consistently.

Slow and steady will win the race.

A Revolutionary Change In Fees

Times have changed.

The financial marketplace has evolved in ways that were difficult to imagine years ago. There has been a major shift in how investments are acquired and how much is paid for buying and selling those transactions.

Thankfully, the process of investing money has shifted to the consumer. We can purchase investments easily with little or no cost. This is fantastic news for consumers and those wanting to retire on time or early, and who want to have the assets in place to do so.

But first, let us go back in time.

One of my favorite investing stories revolves around an individual named Nicolas Darvas. Perhaps you have heard of him or his investing strategies. Darvas was a professional dancer who traveled the world during the 1950s. He was also a self-taught investor who was constantly reading and educating himself when he was not performing. His biggest claim to fame was his strategy that he called "The Box Theory."

The basic principle was based on momentum and volume. It was a little too speculative for my taste, but if you are interested, Darvas wrote an intriguing book called *How I Made 2,000,000 Dollars in the Stock Market* back in 1960. It is a compelling read, but he was also subject to an investigation that his claims could not be substantiated. Proceed at your own risk.

One thing that did catch my attention in the book is the process that Darvas had to go through to purchase and sell his stocks. It was a major undertaking. Often in cities around the world, Darvas had to send all purchase and sale requests to his stockbroker via telegram or cable. It could be several days before he received anything back. He hoped to receive acknowledgment that his trades had been completed somewhere around the price point he was expecting. Trading at that time took lots of effort and cost.

While his techniques are certainly up for debate, his desire to educate himself and jump over major hurdles just to buy and sell stock trades is not. Luckily, we do not have to send telegrams to our broker from overseas just to buy a stock.

Fast-forward to the mid-seventies and eighties. Deregulation of the broker industry was taking place, and the proliferation of discount brokers began. Stockbrokers were able to charge varying commission rates, and competition was born. The names from this time period might sound familiar: Charles Schwab, Dean Witter, and Merrill Lynch.

For investors interested in playing in the stock market, deregulation was a significant event. What cost hundreds of dollars before was now down in the twenties. This shift essentially created a large pool of new investors.

Individuals who might have had an interest in learning and exploring the market often found the entry was cost prohibitive. The invention of discount brokerage along with deregulation changed all that. "Normal people" could own shares in companies with ease.

Today, investment fees are minimal. In many cases, they are zero. I am not certain that word has gotten out to the masses yet.

Many discount brokers today do stock trades for nothing. That includes buying and selling as often as you like. They even allow partial shares to be purchased. If you bought a share of Amazon stock a couple of years ago, you would need to come up with approximately seventeen hundred dollars just to buy one share. Today, you can spend fifty dollars and own part of Amazon.

Why is this change so important?

It's simple. Paying as few fees as possible is critical. The burden for retirement savings has shifted to the individual, so every dollar counts.

1% + 1% = Too Much

In a previous section, the question was asked if your advisor is really advising you.

This section contains that familiar theme but takes it one step further. A great con game is being played with your money. It's not a Ponzi scheme; it's perfectly legal.

It's called assets under management.

Investment advisors have one goal-to get *your* assets under *their* management. The problem is that their business model is at the expense of your financial future.

Let's expand on this further. Every dollar you invest now is worth multiple dollars in the future. When other people are taking those dollars, it sets you back financially.

Here's how it works:

When you turn over your assets to an advisor, they execute the trades on your behalf. Your assets typically go into mutual funds. The mutual fund company charges you to manage those funds called an expense ratio. It is common for this expense ratio to be around 1% or possibly higher.

Next comes your advisor. They charge another 1% to "manage" your funds. Even worse, if your advisor doesn't really care about you, they will invest your money in funds that pay them a commission or a load.

I freely admit that I suck at math. But I understand this.

1% + 1% equals too much.

If I invest $100,000 over twenty years and average an 8% return after the expense ratio is taken out, I have $466,086 at the end.

If I invest $100,000 over twenty years and average an 8% return after the expense ratio is taken out *and I pay my advisor 1%*, I have $386,968 at the end.

$466,086 or $386,968? You choose.

Advisors are not managing your funds; they are holding them. And it costs you lots of money. Pay them for advice, not for looking you up in their computer. Accepting investment advisor fees for assets under management is where many people make a big mistake.

So how is it that I can buy and sell these investments for free, but my financial advisor does not share that information? Because they make their living on your money and depend on your lack of knowledge to do it.

Remember what I mentioned previously: stocks and bonds will go up and down the same regardless of who placed the transaction and who holds it. It just costs you more money if someone does that for you and continually charges you to keep it.

Let's say you reply to one of those "free" offers on the radio to have a new financial advisor look at your current financial picture. They will probably ask you about your goals, and after reviewing your portfolio, they will come up with a strategy. Then, through lots of sales lingo, they are going to ask you to transfer your funds to their company to execute the strategy.

If you are sold, you just gave up a ton of your money.

And your financial advisor is great at reminding you how wonderful this is. "The more you make, the more we make." "If your balance grows, then ours does too." "It is a win-win."

It is not a win-win.

You lose 1-2% of your portfolio every year. That means your money goes into someone else's pocket. It is done quietly.

But for what? So that someone else will place and watch your investments. However, that's something you can do on your home computer anytime you want. Ask your advisor for a statement of the *exact* amount of fees you pay each year. Good luck finding that information.

With all that said, I am not against investment advisors. In fact, I think they are important. However, look at their title: advisor. That is something that may be important to pay for.

Life gets complex, and so does making financial decisions. My theory has always been to pay for advice when needed but execute that advice on my own when it is prudent and simple to do so. Financial advisors advise, you execute the strategy. It is your money, not theirs.

So great, how do I invest in the market?

Most discount brokers have moved to a no-fee, no-commission structure. That means you get to invest for free. Every time you purchase (or sell) your investments, whether they are individual stocks or mutual funds, you incur no additional fees.

The difference between making a 10% return and 8% (because maybe your fees were 2%) is major. It is worth tens of thousands of dollars over time.

Holding *your* money means the financial advisor will be taking those cruises in retirement instead of you.

Buying Cattle

—————◦❦◦—————

The Difference Between the Wealthy and Poor

The difference between becoming wealthy or financially struggling in your life is not complicated.

Creating wealth is not really about the amount of money you make or how perfect your budgeting is. Those things are great, but there are plenty of poor people who are great at both of those.

Wealth is about one thing only: purchasing assets.

People who build wealth focus their energy and spending on acquiring assets. The good news is that this is a simple concept and straightforward to understand.

An asset is something you purchase that creates value: financial value.

In other words, assets make you money. Liabilities do the exact opposite. They take money from your pocket. Learning the difference between an asset and a liability is the first and most critical step in creating wealth.

Assets can be as simple as a checking or savings account that makes interest. Or it can be much more complex, such as buying businesses and commercial real estate.

Most of us purchase assets through our 401(k), individual retirement accounts, or pension plan. These assets are typically held in mutual funds, which pool investors' money to purchase a large selection of stocks and bonds. Others branch out on their own and pick individual stocks and other investments.

Whichever methods we use to purchase investments, we must make choices about how the money is invested. The relationship between risk and reward is a major part of the game. Anytime you purchase an asset, there is always a risk. Everyone has a different tolerance for that risk, and it is critical to figure out what is acceptable to you. Your goal is easy: to get the best return you can generate with as little risk as possible.

That is not always easy. As you can imagine, the promised land lies somewhere in the middle.

For me, the middle lies in stocks that meet a specific pattern over time as well as other income-producing investments such as bonds, real estate investment trusts, and utilities. Investments should not only grow over time but produce income that is reinvested until you need it.

Very few investments can outperform strong dividend stocks. Particularly those that have a history of increasing their dividends over time with those dividends being reinvested.

Discussing assets would be incomplete if we did not address real estate, particularly your home. A question often comes up whether your home is an asset. That depends on who you ask because it can fit both sides of the equation. Many build equity. Others are house poor.

I am on the side of yes, your home is an asset, but only if your mortgage payment allows for disposable income on a regular basis for other investments. Think of your home as something you pay for so you can have shelter, not necessarily as an investment.

Why?

Because like stocks, appreciation should be happening in the background while you focus on generating cash flow through other investments. A home often has value built into it over time, but not simple liquidity. You will always need a place to live. It may not easily convert to money you can live on.

Purchasing Cattle

You may not be literally purchasing cattle, but I will explain the concept.

Perhaps you have heard this phrase before: **"Big Hat, No Cattle."**

In other words, it means a flashy exterior with few assets to back it up. This condition is pervasive within our country. We also know it by the phrase "keeping up with Mr. and Mrs. Jones." In order to have a better financial future and create wealth for yourself, you cannot be like everyone else.

Your path cannot be focused on being image-centric but rather it should follow asset building. This is about your financial future and that of your family. We do not care about the person next door.

This book and the investment strategy in Section Two is all about **"Small Hat, Lots of Cattle."** Financial freedom comes from purchasing assets that produce income.

Focus on creating wealth, build it quietly, and do not advertise until you have made it. The world is full of people who advertise with zero assets.

Be the opposite.

With the extra dollars in your pocket, you have two choices: consumerism (Big Hat) or investing in assets (Cattle). I suggest buying assets that will make you income. The personal satisfaction and the freedom that comes with having wealth outweighs image by a million to one.

Look at everyone around you and how they consume. There are lessons everywhere you look. People who build wealth do not follow the herd. Many times, they watch how most people live in our consumer world and do the exact opposite. They do not attract attention until they have lots of cattle to back it up or are not interested in attention at all, just freedom.

I recently read this from someone who sold cars for a living.

"When selling new cars, I found that the majority of them shouldn't have been — 80% or more. They almost always came in owing more on their trade-ins than they were worth, put down very little cash, and were financially strapped. We called them the 30,000-dollar millionaires."

Big hat, no cattle.

My goal is not to discourage people from buying nice cars. They are just a lot more enjoyable to drive when your wealth or passive income is paying for them.

So, let us figure this out. How do we buy cattle?

It's simple: purchase assets.

Financial assets are things you buy that return money to your pocket, usually over time. That money may be actual cash or something of value that can be sold for cash. There are a lot of options.

The options include stocks and bonds, real estate, businesses, fine wine, fine art, gold, silver, corn, oil, racing horses—and cows, perhaps. Some of these are certainly riskier than others, but all have the potential of producing income.

I favor high-quality, dividend-producing stocks because they meet both requirements: cash flow and value. These stocks are easy to purchase, often at little or no cost.

I am not smart enough to be good at anything else, so I stick to what I know.

Here's another important thought regarding asset building:

People who create wealth collect interest; they do not pay it.

It is a major rule for those who build wealth versus those who struggle. **Interest that you collect is an asset. Interest that you pay is not; it is someone else's asset.**

Later in this book, I describe the importance of being on the right side of the equation. The importance of collecting interest and not paying it is exactly what I am referring to.

What about my budget? How about I just budget my way to riches? If I cut out the Starbucks, I will make it.

No.

Budgeting is an overused financial concept and can be found everywhere. It is not where your focus should be. Your focus should be on buying assets at every opportunity. It is a different mentality. It does not matter where you find the money to invest if you are committed. You will find it because it is worth more than the coffee you drink.

I am not a big believer in the concept of "Rice and Beans, Beans and Rice," if you know what I mean. Debt is certainly an anchor on building assets, but wealth is not necessarily created from starving yourself or your family, in my opinion.

For most individuals, living with a lot less is a failed psychological experiment.

It is sort of like buying the health club membership on January 1st and training for your first marathon, only to load up on Twinkies on the 22nd, and you have only been to the gym three times.

It's a nice idea, but it is nearly impossible to execute when it completely turns your life around 180 degrees. Few people are wired that way and can easily get discouraged. Money flows in and out of your life constantly. Sometimes you have more than usual and sometimes less.

Do not be concerned about the amounts you invest— just invest.

Create Multiple Incomes

Investing is easy. The hard part: you need money to make money.

One of the biggest challenges in building wealth is that money can be hard to find. You have either got to earn it, borrow it, or inherit it.

Borrowing is not a great plan. Your goal in building wealth is to earn interest, not pay it. Inheriting money is a blessing but often comes with difficult news and emotional decisions. Earning money is simply the best option because you have the most control over it. Taking earned income and turning it into passive income that fuels your life is the ultimate financial win.

Most people never realize this, but your income is the single greatest financial asset that you have. That is, until you have enough investment income to replace it.

As previously mentioned, it is difficult to budget your way to riches. I think that it is impractical. Most people will struggle to follow their budget.

It takes a lot of commitment to only eat out once a month. It is like a diet. We're great at starting and not so great at finishing. It is human nature.

That is why so many investment planners suggest automatic payments to your 401(k) or IRA accounts. You do not see the money. It's a great plan that works.

Here is a better one.

The greatest tool to build wealth is to create extra income that is strictly devoted to investments.

This should be in addition to any percentage of your regular salary that you save. There is a hidden blessing that goes along with this approach. There is a much different feeling about working extra to build your financial future. It is very different from working at your job simply to pay your bills.

Start a business, sell items on eBay, or drive for Uber. Do whatever it takes.

There is no need to overdo it.

Working full time is exhausting enough, so choose something simple that is easy to get started. Many online businesses are easy to set up. Just make sure that any extra income you make is always committed to your financial investments.

Be on the Right Side of the Equation

I am not sure if love is a good metaphor, but if you cannot find that someone special in your life, do not fret. Banks love you. They especially love your wallet.

You cannot say you were never wanted.

Banks do a great job at convincing me and you that we are special. We are so trustworthy and financially astute that they are willing to part with their money with ease. This is interesting because they have probably never met any of us.

Imagine: would you loan ten thousand dollars to someone three doors down from you by putting something in their mailbox? Probably not. In the last few weeks, I have been approved for a home equity loan, a boat loan, a home refinance loan, and a "low rate" credit card. I have somehow been deemed "worthy" of these opportunities.

Money is simply given away too easily because it creates massive profits for companies. Banks are nice for your checking account but not the partner you necessarily want when it comes to building wealth.

Let us look at (enter whatever bank name you like here):

The first side of the equation is a simple concept. Banks make enormous profits by loaning your money to other people. They are in the business of creating (or selling) loans that pay them interest. The consumer in us is constantly bombarded with fancy advertisements. Often a loan today is done within seconds with the click of a mouse.

There's nothing wrong with it. It is the basis of capitalism.

Capitalism is great if you are on the correct side of the equation. The side you want to be on is that of a shareholder. You *collect* interest in the form of dividend payments.

If you are a shareholder, you love people who take lots of loans—assuming they can pay for them.

In a roundabout way, they are paying you. The bank makes a profit off people who hold loans and pays a portion of that profit to the stockholders, typically every quarter.

Always try to be on the right side of the capitalism equation. Your goal is to collect interest, not pay it. However, paying interest is not always evil if it is used to pay for an asset. The biggest asset that comes to mind is your home. You pay a lot of interest when you get a mortgage loan from a bank. The benefit is building equity in your home over time. You are paying that interest to make money in the long run.

I do not talk a lot about debt in this book, but you have heard it a million times. Do everything you can to avoid consumer debt.

Credit cards typically carry the highest interest rate (other than payday loans). The average car loan term for a new vehicle is seventy-two months, with eighty-four months on the horizon. Paying a bank six to seven years' worth of interest on something that fully depreciates is financial suicide. So is paying a credit card company 24-28% interest on things you purchase.

Let capitalism make you wealthy, not the other way around.

Wealth vs. Income

If we look at simple definitions, income is the amount of money you report on your tax return. Wealth is the monetary value of everything you own, minus any balances due.

However, there is only one definition that matters when it comes to this difference.

Wealth does not equal income.

In fact, there are many correlations between the two. As income goes up, so should wealth. Yet for lots of American families, this is not the case.

More money typically means you just buy more things. The more things you buy (non-assets), the more expensive your life becomes. The more expensive your life is, the more money you need.

This cycle sucks. Yet people do it over and over and over.

While there is a definition for wealth, remember the definition of "wealthy" is an individual one. There is no one definition that fits. I know people who have never made more than $30,000 a year and consider themselves wealthy. We also know of lottery millionaires who have committed suicide due to financial struggles.

So, what does this mean to you? A lot.

A person who earns $250,000 per year may never achieve financial freedom. A person who earns $40,000 can easily do that. It is all in decision-making. If you earn $40,000, will you be driving a Lexus? Maybe not, but you will achieve something more important, which is the freedom to quit the race if you plan it right.

Does making more money make it easier to become wealthy? Maybe, but it does not matter. You have a simple goal with any extra income that you generate: buy assets.

Psychology of Money

The Psychological Effect of Money

Money and psychology are closely linked and important to understand if you are going to build wealth.

The number one reason millionaires become millionaires is that they focus on it. That is it. It is that simple. Consider the following quote from the fantastic book *The Millionaire Next Door* by Thomas J. Stanley & William D. Danko:

"If your goal is to become financially secure, you'll likely obtain it . . . But if your motive is to make money to spend money on the good life . . . you're never going to make it."

Look inside yourself and consider the things you focus on. If you want to build wealth, get rich, and have a worry-free retirement, it will take commitment. Your commitment to wealth is no different than the commitment of an athlete who does everything it takes to train him or herself to beat the competition.

Your commitment is no different from that of an entrepreneur who succeeded because they focused on learning the ups and downs of the process and how to pivot, not on getting rich quick. You will progress toward what you focus on and what you put your energy into. If wealth is your goal, then your puck had better start moving toward that end of the ice.

There are many books on the psychology of money. It is a great idea to explore the connection in more detail. I like to focus on a few principles that are important to understand.

#1 Spending money creates powerful euphoria.

That is why people enjoy buying things.

Euphoria, however, is always temporary. Most people consider spending and euphoria a reward for all their hard work. That is why restaurants are always packed on a Friday night. It is completely understandable. Our brains love it when we purchase things.

If our discretionary spending is not used to buy assets, we get the same results—nice clothes but no wealth. The cycle repeats over and over. From paycheck to paycheck, the outcome is always predictable.

It is critical that you focus on breaking this cycle.

The cycle will only be broken if you purchase things that produce income.

#2 Losing money is painful.

In fact, losing money is so painful that it costs lots of people a comfortable retirement. In the world of psychology, it is referred to as loss aversion.

It is a major factor in building wealth.

The basic principle is that losses are much more painful than the pleasure of an equivalent gain. We make decisions that help us avoid losing instead of focusing on those that create a return. It means you believe that if you do not act now, you will miss out on something that you may not have the opportunity to get in the future.

This is advertising, and if you get sucked in, your potential at creating wealth erodes. It is a mind game. Evidence of this is everywhere. Most marketing is based on this principle. In fact, people go to great lengths to avoid losing.

Act now; only five spots left; the sale lasts through Friday; 40% off today only.

Black Friday happens every year—guaranteed. The TV will always be on sale, I promise.

Why does this matter?

Appealing to an individual's fear of loss (or missing out) is a major factor in why people struggle to build wealth. The odds in the sales and marketing world are constantly working against you but are easy to overcome. Take the money that everyone is trying to get from you and buy investments. Instead of buying into the marketing game and keeping up with the Joneses, **buy companies that are convincing all your neighbors to buy their stuff.**

Just watch the world around you.

If the Amazon truck stops four times on your street, invest in Amazon. If the line is so busy at Chipotle that it screws your lunch hour, invest in Chipotle. When Apple jacks up the price of the iPhone and people continue buying it, invest in it.

Just make sure the company pays dividends and does so without fail. You will get wealthy. Let your neighbors pay for your future.

#3 Understanding risk

Investing is like a play on stage. The two major actors are risk and aversion.

Risk means you have the potential of making a significant return at the risk of losing money in the short term. Aversion means you leave lots of money on the table, and you will build savings but not wealth. This will make retirement or financial freedom much more difficult.

Think of the difference between being a day trader or commodity trader (high risk) and having a CD or savings account at your local bank (low risk). The risk versus reward difference is night and day.

Everyone has a risk tolerance that they are comfortable with. That is very much an individual decision, and this book (and anyone else's, frankly) cannot make that decision for you. However, it is important to understand the consequences of too much or too little risk.

If you entertain too much risk, you will quickly quit because losing is painful. But if you work with too little risk, you are not actually buying assets that will make you money. Remember: assets put money in your pocket. Sliding money under your mattress or in a savings account at Chase will produce savings but not much more. You must meet in the middle with a slight edge toward risk. That is exactly what The Method is in Section Two.

I like to think of it this way:

You need to have enough risk so that the benefits (return) are visible on a consistent basis. It is one of the reasons I invest for cash flow first. Companies that pay dividends over a period of history will always pay you. Regardless of whether their stock is going up or down or what the market is doing, the company will pay you for owning their shares.

That is positive cash flow.

Positive cash flow is what will give you the motivation to keep investing.

The Wealth of Freedom

What does wealth do for us? It buys freedom. Plain and simple. It opens up your decision-making possibilities.

As I previously mentioned, wealth also buys joy because it consistently grows in a positive direction. Money makes money. It does not necessarily buy happiness. It's important to recognize the difference.

Freedom + Joy.

I can't think of a better goal to shoot for.Unfortunately, in our society, we seem to attach our worth in life (and joy) to financial achievements, not financial wealth.

There is a big difference.

Financial achievements are things that create status from the view outside. They include the high-paying job with perks, the expensive car, the big house, the country club membership, and the new boat. The problem is that financial achievements are fleeting. They are here today and gone tomorrow. As soon as you lose your income, they are all gone.

The focus on financial achievement has great potential of creating pain if that is what drives you. That is, unless you have the freedom and assets to back them up. If you have the freedom and the assets to back up your financial achievements, you are winning the game at a high level.

Freedom is the destination you want—not a specific number in your account. As I mentioned previously, the funny thing about money is that people will always want more. Focus on how you can use your income and assets to create *your* meaning of freedom.

That meaning can only be determined by you, not a financial advisor or a person writing a book.

Maybe you define it as just having the ability to work part time. Maybe you want the freedom of working for yourself and having the assets to pay for health insurance. Maybe your "freedom" is living in a tiny home and quitting the race for good. You are going to need assets to replace income. Having the ability to replace your income in a passive or semi-passive manner equals freedom to me.

I would be happy to get to that destination.

If This Is Your Worry, You Might Not Make It

I will keep this one short and sweet.

If you worry about the amount of money you make, you will not make it. Again, it is a game of psychology. Without question, this is a difficult statement to make considering the financial pressure that people are under.

Why do I stress the psychology of money so much? Because if you want to be wealthy, it is everything.

Remember, on the opposite side of the coin are salespeople and marketers. They win because everything they do is based on convincing you, through your mind, that you need something, or you are missing out. People who build riches understand that and use psychology in their favor. They understand the game—the game of people and companies whose everyday existence is getting money from your pocket into theirs.

I'll reiterate a couple of points. Capitalism is a great thing if we are on the right side of the equation. We all have things to pay for. We all have decisions to make with our money. That's normal. However, it is amazing when we own the companies that everyone else plows their money into through massive consumerism. The United States is full of them. It is a huge benefit to you if you own the assets that consistently receive their money.

To put this in another way, you create wealth for yourself and your family on the backs of people who spend. Perhaps that sounds mean, but it is simply the flow of capitalism. Like I have mentioned previously, capitalism is not going away.

If you are going to succeed financially, you need to take part in our financial system—whether you agree with it or not.

Here is a simple example.

The next time you pull up to a red light and a Land Rover or Mercedes is next to you, think of the two options. Hopefully, that person understands how the game is played. They made the correct moves and arrived at a place in their lives where luxury things are an easy option, if desired.

That's wonderful for them and bad for you. But more than likely, that is not the case. The "owner" of that Mercedes or Land Rover is not the person driving. The owner is a bank or lending institution. The person driving it looks good. The person who owns stock in the bank that is collecting the money looks better.

And you can own stock in those types of companies regardless of the amount that you make at your job. You just need to be a careful consumer and a smart buyer of assets with the extra income that you have.

Beware of Information Overload

Financial information can be very confusing. There is just too much of it, and it all leads in fifty different directions.

A simple education is all people really need. Too much

information can easily lead to mistakes, including the big ones: fear and overconfidence. It is great to read and educate yourself on financial topics. Most people are very interested in money. Learn as much as you can. But here is my advice: focus on five things.

1. Learn the difference between an asset and a liability.
2. Understand the difference between passive and active investing (passive strategies win).
3. Think psychology. Control over your emotions and the decisions you make (investing versus consumerism) are the difference between those who build wealth and those who remain poor.
4. Know who financial salespeople are, where they disguise themselves, and what their motives are. Remember, to build wealth, you must keep people out of your pocket.
5. Learn how to invest at the minimal cost possible. It is a major factor you control.

Very few people, including professional wealth managers, beat the market over time. That is the big reason I focus on cash flow; it is much more of a guarantee. Granted, my portfolio will move up and down with the market, but like the market itself, it will go up over time. I am not interested in the day-to-day movement of my accounts. It does not matter.

I am interested in the companies I own continuing to

pay dividends on a consistent basis, at a rate that stays the same or increases. I only sell a stock if it decreases its dividend payment, or worse yet, stops altogether.

It makes life very easy from an investment standpoint.

Know What Your Enough Is

Of all the items discussed in these principles, this could certainly be one of the most important. How much is enough? If you cannot answer that, experts say you will never get to the finish line.

Here is the funny thing about money: everyone always wants more of it.

It is difficult for most people to determine what their final number is. Unfortunately, I do not have a magic formula to offer you or a nice "Method." I wish I did. This is a question that many people struggle with.

I am very confident in the strategy of investing that you will find in this book, but not so much in determining what the exact finish line is.

However, I do believe in simplicity.

If you never view it like that, what constitutes enough may be a never-ending question. Everywhere I look, "experts" say you need one million dollars, three million dollars, and so on. These are astronomical numbers for most people.

Suze Orman says everyone needs at least five million dollars to retire. Really? That's not accurate. No wonder people do not make a strong effort to invest for their futures. It appears to be a lost cause and can be incredibly discouraging. Most of us are not in the 1%. It is simply not realistic.

Getting wealthy has a big mental component to it. Master the mental game, and you will have success in building wealth. Goals are great. In fact, goals are important for a lot of things, including investing.

But what if we do not meet our goals or have significant periods where money is flying out of the door. Will you quit?

Here is how I have approached this: just consistently invest. Invest for your future until the day you retire or when you have decided "your river has overflowed" (as I described in the previous section).

Sometimes investments will be in small amounts because that is how life is. Sometimes money comes in more often than expected. Invest big when that happens. It is a good enough finish line. In the end, I cannot tell you how much you will have. There are too many factors. I can guarantee you will have more than you expected, and you will be able to supplement any additional payments you have earned, such as Social Security.

It is about making investing a habit, having a simple

method to follow, and avoiding bad decisions that humans easily make.

Time to Fly

Beware of Green Echoes

Having been a pilot for thirty years, I never worried too much about green echoes on the radar. Typically, all this meant was light rain and probably a smooth trip. Sometimes there was occasional turbulence, but nothing exciting.

A late afternoon over New Mexico at 24,000 feet changed my mind.

When we departed Albuquerque for Phoenix, the weather ahead of us was not particularly concerning. There were puffy clouds and a small chance of rain showers—common for the Southwest during late summer. Climbing out of about 15,000 feet, a thunderstorm cell caught our attention south of Gallup. It was not severe, but it was building.

Given the fact that the airway we were on was fifty nautical miles north of the storm, I did not feel like any diversion was necessary. The radar was just painting light green echoes. Flying in green echoes is part of everyday life for a pilot in the spring and summer.

As we climbed out of 20,000 feet, things started to get interesting.

We went into the clouds. That's completely normal under instrument flight, but the visible world disappears in light green echoes. Within about three minutes, I heard one of the worst things I think a pilot can hear—hail striking the aircraft while flying at roughly 320 miles an hour. The sound is deafening and unmistakable. It is the sound of a pilot's career ending.

Rendering a multimillion-dollar airframe useless in a matter of seconds is not good. I would take an engine failure over this any day.

The only option is to truck on, continue climbing, and hope it does not last. The damage could already be done.

When we arrived in Phoenix, the exit from the cockpit was quick. It was sort of the point of no return. As I walked around the aircraft, I could not find any damage on the airframe, engine inlets, or control surfaces. The plane was in the same condition as when we left Albuquerque, albeit a lot cleaner.

It appeared my saving grace was that we'd encountered rain falling so heavily it sounded like hail. I learned a new respect for green echoes.

So, what does this have to do with investing? Plenty.

Green echoes are essentially just a sense of security. We tend to live for today and expect things to be fine in the future. When it comes to building wealth, a lot of people live in "light rain" but are flying toward yellow and red.

Most of the time, things in our lives go well. Our trip is fairly smooth, with a few bouts of turbulence here and there. In general, we are living in the green echo. Not clear and a million, as pilots love to say on a clear day, but not bad. We get used to our routine. The autopilot is on. Nothing exciting is happening, and everything seems to be going as planned.

But a hailstorm is coming.

Here are two of the most serious echoes we are currently flying around:

Social Security and Defined Benefit Plans (Pensions)

Let us break down the issues.

Social Security is a book on its own, so I will not go that far. There are tons of options for information as well as tons of opinions on this topic. I will leave the heavy lifting to the experts and those who really like to dig in.

I prefer to keep it simple and look at two major

challenges.

First, Social Security was built to supplement income in retirement. It was never designed to fully support retired Americans. It did not work out as planned. Currently, it is the only source of income for an estimated 40-50% of retirees.

The future looks bleak. If no changes are made, the system will run through its reserve assets by 2035. Options are painful all the way around.

I would put my money on a couple of things in the coming years. We will see a change in the benefit formula. If you are tired of working, you will need to take a lower amount (probably much lower) if you want to start collecting Social Security at a reasonable age. Or you'll be waiting and waiting. Starting retirement at age seventy-two is not my plan and hopefully will not be yours.

We'll see changes in taxes again, in the wrong direction. Social Security will need to be funded by raising the amount that is withheld from working individuals. Middle-class Americans will pay the price for this.

Simply put, Social Security just is not enough. In fact, *Forbes* magazine says it best: *Yes, you can live on Social Security if staying alive is your goal.*

Let's move on to pensions. You may be lucky to have one or not. It depends somewhat on who holds your pension and how poorly it is managed. Many pensions are not sustainable without significant reductions.

Unfortunately, you are at the mercy of officials and investment advisors in corporate suits who will decide your financial future.

Even though you have paid into the system all your working life, you will have no voice in how this plays out. You are essentially a pawn in a massive financial game. They get to roll the dice every time while you sit on the sidelines, waiting for your pawn to move backward. Lots of people get rich with pension plans, but the employee is not one of those people.

If you have a pension, you should prepare for significant reductions to your future income. Or you could be worse off and not have a pension at all. Look at Illinois, Kentucky, California. If you are really feeling up for it, take a gander at the Central States Pension Plan.

There is nothing fair about this.

Every time they asked for your money, they got it out of your paycheck. When it is time for you to get paid, someone else will decide that for you. Many pension plans have made promises they will never be able to deliver on. Add in the high levels of mismanagement plus unacceptable risk, and the challenge becomes even greater.

The biggest benefit to a pension is that a lot of people

behind the scenes get rich at your expense. Simply Google "hefty investment fees for pension funds." That is your money just flowing into their pockets. I suggest having a libation in your hand when you do that Internet search.

Where does all of this leave us?

Our number one priority is recognizing the green echoes that may be hazardous to our financial future. Remember: the green echoes are the things that we think will work out as planned. For many Americans, this will not be the case financially.

Second, you must plot and execute a course that will result in financial freedom—**one that you control.** We need to plot the proper course as we dodge the financial "weather cells" on life's radar.

The Method Investor strategy in the second part of this book will show you how to plot and execute your course: a path to financial freedom.

Five Hazardous Attitudes

Pilots are taught early on about hazardous attitudes and the danger they present to safety. Hopefully, our safety is not at risk while we are investing, but these hazardous attitudes can certainly be financially damaging.

Although they are not particularly related, there is an interesting correlation between these two passions. It is worth a comparison.

Attitudes that are hazardous to investing:

Anti-Authority

This is a common one.

There are times in life when we act as if the rules do not apply to us, even if we refuse to admit it or simply do not recognize it. Psychology plays a significant part in this as well. The more we do it and get away with it, the more confidence we have that we must play outside the rules. The problem is that it will eventually catch up with us, and the outcome is often disastrous.

Aviation is full of regulations, and for good reason. Pilots are required to know them verbatim and often must demonstrate their knowledge during testing events to continue their employment and satisfy the Federal Aviation Administration. Safety comes from everyone staying within the limitations of their aircraft and the federal aviation laws.

For investors, there are not too many laws that govern our investment strategies. Outside of insider trading and pyramid schemes, we should be in good shape.

However, there are basic principles for success. It is not a bad idea to think of them as "laws."

1. Pay yourself first. Always.
2. Invest, do not speculate.

3. Focus long term, not short. Great companies have a proven record over time and pay their shareholders; invest in them.
4. Success in investing comes from discipline.

We do not need to be a financial planner to be successful at building wealth. One of the greatest determinants is wanting to chase ways to get rich quickly. It does not happen that way. Keep it simple. Stay within the basic laws of investing, and you will win the game.

Invulnerability

We tend to believe that bad things will not happen to us.

Think about it this way: if you really believed that every time you got in a car you were going to be seriously injured or killed, it would be tough to turn the key. A certain amount of invulnerability allows us to live our life, and that is a good thing.

However, there is a fine line. The more invulnerable we feel, the more dangerous life becomes. Good judgment begins to go out the door. We overcome that in flying, and driving for that matter, by being cautious and having structure around what we are doing.

When it comes to our financial situation, lots of people believe things will just work out. While this may be true, they will not work out the way you want them to. We still need to plan for our future and realize it is not going to happen for us.

Macho

This is perhaps my favorite one to discuss because I have seen it so many times.

I have trained a lot of pilots over the years. I would take a hundred "C" students with a great attitude and a willingness to learn over an "A" pilot who has fantastic stick skills but the recklessness and cockiness to get everyone killed.

Aviation accident reports are unfortunately littered with examples of this attitude. It is amazing how prevalent it really is. If you are interested in aviation, look at the Czar 52 military accident. It is a tragic story that absolutely highlights the dangers of overconfidence.

Of course, it is very difficult to compare the heartbreaking outcome of an aviation accident to investing but doing so provides a simple lesson. In investing, heartbreaking financial outcomes often come from overconfidence. The stories associated with people trying to strike it rich in a short period of time are everywhere.

In fact, a recent story surfaced that involved a twenty-year-old who committed suicide; his death was apparently brought on by short selling securities. Very few people are financial professionals, and most of them are right only some of the time.

I like this recent quote from the Costco CEO:

"On Wall Street, they're in the business of making money between now and next Thursday. I don't say that with any bitterness, but we can't take that view. We want to build a company that will still be here in 50 to 60 years."

There's nothing reckless about this statement. It expresses a goal and a great point to focus on. These are the types of companies you want to invest in. Ultimately, you can breathe a sigh of relief. You do not need to be an A student when it comes to investing.

Impulsivity

This is the danger of doing things too quickly. Unfortunately, I have seen this up close and personal in an airplane.

I was giving a flight test to a pilot so they could continue to be qualified for their pilot position. There is a requirement to shut down one engine so the pilot can demonstrate the ability to secure the "failed" engine and continue flying on the operating engine. The pilot flying not only neglected to secure the engine I cut, but quickly reached up and cut the fuel to the only engine operating. Being in a two-engine airplane with both engines silent 1,000 feet above the ground was not part of the plan.

It was a scary lesson in the dangers of being impulsive.

Pilots are often taught that when something goes wrong in an airplane, the first thing to do is "wind your watch." That means: fly the airplane first and think before you act.vWhen it comes to investing, impulsivity is a great way to lose money.

It is all too common.

Some examples include following a "hot tip," investing in a stock because it is hitting new highs and thinking there is no way it can stop, watching cable television investment rock stars at 7 p.m. and placing your newest trade by 8 p.m.

Day trading has become all the rage, but it is the definition of impulsivity. Roughly 95% of day traders eventually lose all of their money in the market. These are not the odds you are looking for—super exciting but super expensive.

Overcoming impulse investing is easy. You must follow fundamentals; invest in companies that dominate their market with a history of paying dividends over time. Second, fund your account as often as possible. That is it.

Resignation

This is the one we must be the most careful of when it comes to investing. It is too easy to do. If we fall into the resignation trap, we do not really see any need to invest or we just give up. In other words, we think, "What is the use? I do not have the knowledge, money, or time."

You need to get past this type of thinking. There is nothing difficult or unique about building wealth. It is just a process. Media fuels the problem of resignation. If all of us need three million dollars to retire, maybe resignation does not look so bad.

In simulation training, pilots face every imaginable emergency. Things are not left to fate. Pilots prepare for the possibilities so we can control the outcome when problems arrive.

This is also a great lesson for investing. You do not want to leave things to fate. You control your financial future and freedom. Focus on the commitment to building wealth. If I retire with an extra $30,000 dollars, then I am $30,000 dollars richer when I retire. It all counts.

Area 51

This is an area in the middle of Nevada where experimental military activities take place. If you are into national security or UFOs, this is your place.

If you are into investing, this is not your place. There are a lot of Area 51s in the financial business—things that are out of the norm or places where people lose a lot of money.

Here are my Area 51s:

#1: Day trading

Quitting your job because somebody on YouTube convinced you that you are the second coming of Paul Tudor Jones is not a good strategy. It is flashy, exciting, emotional, and very expensive.

It is estimated that only 2% of day traders turn a profit. Not only will you lose money with many stock picks you hold, but Uncle Sam will also slap you with heavy taxes on the ones that you do win. It's a double whammy that you should avoid.

#2 Short selling

This one is intriguing.

It is basically betting that a stock will lose value instead of going up. I like to equate it to throwing dice at a craps table in Las Vegas and betting the Do Not Pass line. You are betting against the shooter.

Short selling sounds nice in theory because stocks lose value all the time. Here is the problem: your losses can be unlimited. If you buy $1,000 of Apple stock, the worst that can happen is that you lose $1,000.

If you short $1,000 of Apple stock hoping that it declines, your risk is phenomenal. Let us say for fun that two days after shorting the stock, Apple announces a new product that was being kept under the radar. Excitement builds, everyone wants the stock, and the price shoots through the roof.

You are screwed. You might feel like heading out to Area 51 for real, catching one of those rocket ships, and getting the hell out of Dodge. You will continue to owe the difference between your purchase and the climbing stock. Your loss grows as the stock grows, and who knows where it will end. You'd better hope you have deep pockets.

I like to sleep at night. Short selling: no thanks.

#3 Options

This is the hot item right now, and it sounds great. I pay a small fee now to watch what a stock will do. I have the right (or option) to purchase it if I want or punt and say no thank you within a specified time frame. It is like buying a little insurance policy before committing to a stock purchase.

Awesome options take my risk away, and I am going to get rich. Not exactly.

With stock options, you are basically using leverage. You're spending a small sum to win a larger sum. Leverage equals risk because things happen twice as fast— gains *and* losses. Plus, you are paying for the privilege of watching on the sidelines. It adds up to a lot of money. And because options have a time frame, you must exercise it when it comes due whether you want to or not. If you purchase a stock outright, you control when you sell it. You can own it for four days or forty years.

It is easier on your heart to buy assets on a regular basis and hold them long term. It is also easier on your wallet.

#4 Buying on Margin

This is borrowing money at a certain rate and hoping that you can invest it, make money on the borrowed money, then pay it back—hopefully, with a profit. Good luck.

My issue with this one is simple. The goal is to collect interest, not pay it. Pros struggle to pick stocks correctly. There is so much risk, especially with borrowed money.

It's all too much heartburn for me. I will pass.

#5 Salespeople

Big Area 51. Watch like a hawk.

Remember, everyone is trying to get your money into their pockets. The financial business is full of salespeople, both legal and illegal. They do not always have your best interest at heart. More than likely, they have their own interests prioritized (or their sales manager's).

Do not freely give your money away because of shiny things you see in advertising. *Always attach value to what you are paying for.*

I am not anti-salesperson. I just understand it is a mental game of separating money from one to another. It is worth it if the value is worth it.

This book can be used as a simple example.

If you purchased this book for $10 and one piece of information in it led to you purchasing assets, you win. The value is much greater than what you spent. If you have been investing for years, understand the pitfalls, and can tell the difference between an asset and a liability, your $10 might be better spent elsewhere.

Simple wins the race. Keep your investment strategy basic and control the things you can control, like discipline, commitment to building wealth, and paying minimal fees.

At the end of the day, do not be a test pilot. Leave that excitement to the real Area 51.

Ben Franklin and Tijuana Tacos

Move Over, Warren Buffett, Enter Ben Franklin

Warren Buffett is the most talked about and most referenced investor in history. And for good reason.

Perhaps the person who should be first is Benjamin Franklin.

Most people know him as one of the founding fathers of the United States or perhaps for a kite, a key, and the flow of electricity. His knowledge of money was extraordinary, particularly for the time.

Ben Franklin was truly an amazing person. In addition to being an inventor, philosopher, scientist, and diplomat, he was a writer. He wrote a book called *Poor Richard's Almanac,* and within that writing was an essay named "The Way to Wealth." It is amazing to think that a simple essay written in 1758 would be valid today. It very much is. In fact, these quotes from the essay say it all:

"But with our industry we must likewise be steady, settled, and careful, and oversee our own affairs with our own eyes, and not trust too much to others; . . . Trusting too much to others' care is the ruin of many; for in the affairs of this world men are saved, not by faith, but by the want of it . . ."

Another valuable one ...

"A ploughman on his legs is higher than a gentleman on his knees, as Poor Richard says. . . But this they might have known before, if they had taken his advice. If you would know the value of money, go and try to borrow some; for, he that goes a borrowing goes a sorrowing, as Poor Richard says . . ."

In other words, everyone wants your money. Keep people out of your pocket. And secondly, stay out of debt. What worked in 1758 works today. The philosophy around building wealth does not change. Franklin's simple essay was not the only gift he offered to those who wanted to build wealth.

He also delivered an amazing financial lesson in his final years. Less than a year before his death in 1790, he added an addendum to his will. He bequeathed $1,000 each to the cities of Boston and Philadelphia (in today's terms, those amounts would be worth approximately $100,000 each).

Both gifts were held in trust, which required each city

to gather interest on the amounts for 200 years. The cities were expected to loan money to young apprentices to learn job skills and to those interested in opening their own business. Each city stuck to the promises contained in the will and continued to grow their funds. They did, however, have to adapt to the current times. For instance, Boston has used their fund to loan money to roughly 7,000 medical students since 1960.

The experiment ended in 1990 at the end of 200 years. Boston and Philadelphia were required to empty the funds and were free to spend the money as they chose.

Starting with $1,000 each, here was the official tally:

Boston's account was worth five million dollars, and Philadelphia's account was worth two million dollars. (Yes, it appears that Boston did a much better job of managing their money.) Where did the money go? Boston used it to establish a trade school, The Franklin Institute of Boston. Philadelphia used their money toward scholarships for local high school students.

It's such an amazing story that has simple implications for those who want to build wealth. It underscores the importance of collecting interest, reinvesting that interest, and, most critically, watching that interest compound over time.

Granted, we are not going to be able to spend our nest egg at the end of 200 years, but the principle is what counts. Time matters. If you have not started investing, begin now. If you have started, focus on adding as many assets to your accounts as possible.

Just do it. Do not be concerned about the day-to-day movement of the market. Great financial advice from a truly incredible American.

Tijuana Fish Tacos

If anyone has ever ventured into Tijuana, Mexico, investing is probably not the first thing that comes to mind.

Tijuana is famous (or infamous) for lots of things. Charles Schwab is not one of them.

In fact, from the corner of Avenida Revolucion and Calle Benito Juarez, you are 2,771 miles from Wall Street. Admittedly, it is an odd place to find investment advice. It was on that corner many years ago that I picked up on a valuable lesson.

Growing up in Southern California, heading to Tijuana with friends was sort of a rite of passage. Nightclubs, 80s music, tequila poppers, and Marines on leave from Camp Pendleton were all part of the scene. It was general chaos with a small amount of debauchery.

But there was also food.

Particularly, there were street vendors selling anything

they had. Although their dishes were often disguised by the words "hot dogs" or "fish tacos," it was food, nonetheless. By two in the morning, these items looked a lot more appetizing than they should have.

I found my way to one of those fish taco stands one Saturday night.

I never caught the name of the owner, but I recall him as friendly and slightly disheveled. He spoke little English, and I was talented at broken Spanish, especially at this time in the morning, so the transaction went smoothly. I ordered three tacos. Luckily, most taco stands in Tijuana took US dollars, and I proceeded to pay him three dollars and fifty cents. He promptly took the dollar bills and put them in his right pocket. He then took the fifty cents and put that in his left pocket.

Clearly, he was a lot more weighed down on his left side as his pocket was bulging with change. It looked worn out and ready to rain money on the streets of TJ. I figured it was some sort of simple way of accounting or making change.

"*Esta es para mis hijos.*" This is for my kids, he said.

After a little more curiosity and digging in, I found that he had been doing this for nearly twenty years. The dollar bills went into running the fish stand, and the change was for his future. He took the change from his pocket every day and began filling those old, large Arrowhead water bottles. I am sure over twenty-some years that it added up.

The simple lesson of this father running his fish taco stand and preparing for his future has never been lost on me. It should not be lost on you either. It is a lesson of paying yourself first.

We can easily follow this path and invest our "change" every day—thankfully, for a much greater return than a jar will give us.

I do not suggest you rush out and sink down some of Tijuana's famous "fish tacos." That alone could be hazardous to your retirement.

Just follow in the footsteps of the chef.

Section II

❧

The Method Investment Strategy

Introduction

This section outlines The Method investment strategy.

It is a method of picking stocks that meet a specific criterion and have a strong history of paying investors cash. It is a simple step-by-step process that takes minimal time to complete.

A few notes:

There are a lot of ways to invest money. This is one of them. Whichever way you choose to invest, be sure it fits your goals and emotional stamina (risk tolerance). Some people will risk everything for the excitement of a fast gain. Others are so conservative that you might as well bury the money and let inflation dig it up and steal it.

The Method meets risk in the middle. It involves enough risk to make a good return and enough diversification and protection to ride out the market downturns.

It is designed to supplement other existing retirement plans that you might have. This could include Social

Security, 401(k)s, IRAs, government pensions, etc.

The objective of the strategy is to invest in high-quality, dividend-paying stocks for the purpose of supplementing your monthly income (cash flow) during retirement, while building capital appreciation over time. Human error is what leads people to lose their potential at wealth. Emotion takes over, and financial mistakes are made. Many people simply sell at the wrong time.

The Method is designed to avoid these pitfalls.

Once you have completed the steps and picked your investments, add money and watch it grow. The Method strategy will result in twenty to forty stocks in your portfolio that you hold long term.

The only time you sell a stock is if it no longer pays dividends. It puts your portfolio on autopilot with consistent cash payments.

It is beneficial to track your monthly cash dividend payments. Why? Because they always go up. Seeing your cash flow constantly moving in a positive direction will motivate you to continue adding money to your investments.

Over time, very few investments can beat the returns of high-quality dividend stocks with dividends reinvested until needed for income.

I do not pick your stocks or tell you what to buy. You do. It is your portfolio. I just help with the road map to get there.

The Method Explained

The Method investment strategy is straightforward to execute. It consists of doing research, purchasing investments, and holding them long term.

The strategy is designed to be completed in multiple steps.

The research consists of finding stocks that meet a specific criterion. Although no investment is guaranteed, this criterion ensures we have the best opportunity to create cash flow and financial growth. Picking your stocks is as simple as looking them up on a computer and applying some basic rules.

It has become much easier for individuals to purchase shares of stock. Everything can be done online with the click of a mouse. It does not take any special knowledge or skill.

Holding your investments long term, however, is not easy. It is an emotional challenge. There is always something to pay for.

Your freedom and wealth should be at the top of the list. Holding your investments long term and reinvesting the cash you make from them is a big part of the road map.

The Method Investor website

In order to assist you in completing the steps, visit the website:

www.themethodinvestor.com

There is additional information, including a simple, online class with videos that will help you complete the steps.

The Method Steps

—————— ❦ ——————

The Method Investor – Step #1   Finding Stocks

Find dividend stocks with the following characteristics:

Dividend yield between 3.0% and 5.5%

Three point zero is the minimum yield to gain passive income and outgrow inflation. Higher yields carry risk that the value of the stock is in decline, or the company will reduce dividends, or worse, not continue to pay dividends. I limit yield to 5.5%.

Market capitalization above one billion

Companies with market capitalization above one billion are very attractive because of their stability and the ability to pay dividends on a consistent basis. These companies also tend to dominate their competition.

Beta at or below 1.00

Beta represents the volatility of a certain stock. Does the stock price stay steady when the market moves, or does it have wild ups and downs?

This is a critical part of a stock you pick. If you are going to build steady dividend wealth, you need a portfolio that can ride out downturns in the stock market. Beta ratings at one or below will allow you to sleep at night.

The Method Investor – Step #2   Make list of stocks

Generating the list of stocks you will invest in will involve paring down your initial stock list to roughly seventy to eighty stocks.

Using the criteria in Step #1, you will typically generate a list of 300-400 stocks. This seems like a lot, but it will be easy to reduce. Our goal is to pare it down to a list of seventy to eighty stocks that we can further evaluate.

Choose companies that are familiar to you

Go through your list and pick the companies that are familiar to you. These may be companies that you know or have just heard of. There is no rocket science to this. It is important that you invest in companies you know and somewhat understand.

Think Coca-Cola or Walmart instead of some gas company in Brazil. If you are curious, copy the stock symbol and search it in your browser to learn more. Often you will be familiar with it if it is an American company.

Avoid stocks that are not listed on the NYSE or Nasdaq

In step #1, each of those stocks has an exchange that they are traded on. You want companies listed on the New York Stock Exchange (NYSE) or Nasdaq. Avoid OTC.

New list of stocks

The completed work above will produce a list of about seventy to eighty stocks. You might have a little less or a little more than that. This is perfectly fine. In the next step, we will take your new list and determine which ones have a long history of paying cash to their stockholders.

The Method Investor – Step #3　Verify Dividend History

This is the most important piece of The Method. These are the companies that are going to pay for your future. We must make sure they have a significant history of paying cash to shareholders and will most likely continue doing this in the future.

Finding the dividend history of a company

Using your new list of seventy or so stocks, begin looking for their dividend history. We are looking for at least a five-year history of increasing dividend payments over time. At the very least, we want this to be even over time without any declines. A longer span (ten years, etc.) can show this even better.

Your ultimate list

This process should get you down to your ultimate list of about twenty to forty stocks. Twenty should be the minimum so that you are fully diversified across multiple sectors of the economy. Above forty is reasonable if your stocks meet the criteria.

Note: *More information finding the dividend history of companies, including good websites, can be found on www.themethodinvestor.com*

The Method Investor – Step #4   Your Brokerage Account

Here is where we take the work we have done and put it into action. In order to buy the companies that you have chosen, you will need to open a brokerage account to purchase the shares.

Choosing a broker for your account

There are multiple options that you can choose for your account. When choosing a broker, make sure they offer the following:

Free investing

The ability to purchase partial shares of stock

Low minimums to get started and low amounts for additional investment

Automatic reinvestment of dividends

Automatic rebalancing of your account with each purchase

Easy to use, modern user interface on all devices

Registered with FINRA and a member of SIPC

Note: *Brokerage accounts may be set up in different ways: Individual, Joint, Traditional IRA, Roth IRA, etc. These are questions for a financial advisor or lawyer.*

Please consult with one if you need further information.

The success of The Method (and your wealth) is dependent upon these elements.

The Method Investor – Step #5   Feed Your Account

Make every effort to invest money into your account constantly. Money grows on money, particularly with dividend investing.

More Shares = More Cash Flow

Understanding the importance of purchasing assets

Instead of money going out of your pocket, you are buying assets that put money in your pocket. This is critical if you are going to be financially independent. Each time you purchase additional stocks, you are building your future

Investment amounts

Do not get caught up in the amounts you are investing. Just do it as often as possible—twenty dollars here, fifty there. Over time, it is truly impressive how your account will grow. It all adds up.

Remember the water analogy. It starts as a dripping faucet and ends up a river that overflows its banks. The water never even turns on if you do not act.

Passive income

When you get paid dividends (cash) from the

companies you own, it is completely passive. You did not have to work for the cash that the company is paying you. You simply get paid because you own part of the company.

This is where you want to be.

The Method Investor – Step # 6   Charting Your Progress

This step is completely optional but very valuable. Setting up a simple chart in Google Sheets or Excel is an excellent way to track your cash flow.

As I have mentioned, investing is a game of emotion. When you focus on the right things, you will be successful.

As your account grows, so will your dividend income. Watching this happen though the use of a chart will keep you positive on your progress regardless of market swings.

It's simple. Here is how to do it:

Every month, go to your brokerage account activity and search "dividends."

Add the totals for each month.

Put the figures in an Excel spreadsheet or Google Sheets (Google Sheets is free). I recommend using the option of line graph with markers to display your amounts.

Enter your totals for each month and watch your monthly income rise.

Patience is key with investing, including The Method. Your cash flow will start small, but will grow with all the dividends you reinvest and the deposits you make to your account. <u>Focus on Step #5.</u>

Note: Dividend payments are typically paid quarterly; some are monthly. Your monthly cash flow will vary because of this. For example, dividends tend to be heaviest in December and lower in January.